Flavours of Wales

THE WELSH LAMB COOKBOOK

Gilli Davies and Huw Jones

GRAFFEG

The Welsh Lamb Cookbook
Published in Great Britain in 2017 by
Graffeg Limited

Text by Gilli Davies copyright © 2017.
Photographs by Huw Jones copyright © 2017.
Food styling by Paul Lane.
Designed and produced by Graffeg Limited
copyright © 2017.

Graffeg Limited, 24 Stradey Park Business
Centre, Mwrwg Road, Llangennech, Llanelli,
Carmarthenshire SA14 8YP Wales UK
Tel 01554 824000 www.graffeg.com

Gilli Davies is hereby identified as the author of
this work in accordance with section 77 of the
Copyrights, Designs and Patents Act 1988.

A CIP Catalogue record for this book is
available from the British Library.

ISBN 9781912050277

1 2 3 4 5 6 7 8 9

CONTENTS

4 Introduction to Welsh Lamb

6 Welsh Lamb with Plums in Pastry

10 Salt Marsh Welsh Lamb Baked with Potatoes

14 Welsh Lamb Shanks with Thyme

18 Welsh Spring Lamb with Asparagus

22 Slow Roast Welsh Lamb with a Mustard Glaze

26 Loin of Welsh Lamb in a Crisp Roll

30 Welsh Lamb Chops with Crushed Minted Peas

34 Skewers of Welsh Lamb

38 Butterflied Welsh Lamb on the Barbecue

42 Lamb Guard of Honour with Rosemary and Port Sauce

46 Metric and Imperial Equivalents

47 Welsh Cookbooks by Gilli Davies

48 Flavours of Wales Collection

Welsh Lamb

Mountain lamb is sweet, valley lamb is fatter,
I therefore deemed it meet, to carry off the latter!

"The leg of mutton of Wales beats the leg of mutton of any other country, and I had never tasted a Welsh leg of mutton before. Certainly I shall never forget that first Welsh leg of mutton which I tasted, rich but delicate, replete with juices derived from the aromativ herbs of the noble Berwyn, cooked to a turn, and weighing just four pounds", wrote George Borrow in *Wild Wales*, 1862.

But why should Welsh lamb taste so different, and better than any other? Is it the breed or the feed, or perhaps the environment in which it is reared?

A combination of all three must be the answer.

Some of the Welsh breeds of sheep are among the oldest in the world, and they still form a major part of sheep farming in Wales. This is due to their resilience, good grazing abilities, fine mothering and value for money to the farmer.

Herbage plays a large part too. Sheep reared on the salt marshes have the benefit of grazing delicious coastal flavours, such as samphire and other wild and salty herbs, whereas no grass can be lusher than that of the sheltered lowland valleys of Wales. Then up on the mountains, the heathers, wild berries and herbs will bring a different flavour to the meat.

As for the environment, whether the sheep graze in the valleys, wind-swept coasts, or the mountains and uplands, the air is clear, the grass is pure and the environment is much the same as it has been for centuries. So perhaps the quality of the much-praised Welsh lamb can be attributed to its slow maturing over a longer period on natural foodstuffs.

Top quality Welsh lamb is available just about all the year round now, with lowland spring lamb ready for Easter, lamb reared along the coastal plains available throughout the summer months and mountain lamb coming into the shops towards the end of the summer. So it's all down to choice really. Easter lamb will be tender but may not have the strongest flavour, salt marsh lamb is tender and tasty, but for me, I like to choose mine later in the summer, when the lamb really tastes of lamb. Just right for a roast, barbecue or rib-sticking casserole.

Lamb is versatile too. Delicate spring lamb is available before mint appears in the garden and that may be a good thing, for mint sauce may just be overpowering. Why not stick to seasonal accompaniments, such as asparagus or young peas and beans? Mid-summer, nothing tastes better on the barbecue than a butterflied leg of lamb, marinated in summer herbs, grilled pink in the middle and crisp on the outside. For those long winter nights, what could be more comforting than a casserole of lamb shanks in rich gravy?

WELSH LAMB WITH PLUMS IN PASTRY

Autumn is the best time to eat upland lamb, when it has had the summer to mature on a diet of good grass and natural herbs. It teams up really well with the autumn glut of plums. This dish also makes a great party piece, a huge mound of golden pastry encasing succulent lamb and delicious sweet plums with a fruity sauce.

WELSH LAMB WITH PLUMS IN PASTRY

Ingredients

1.5-2kg leg of lamb, boned or shoulder (with excess fat cut away)

225g red plums, stoned and chopped (Victoria plums for preference)

1 garlic clove, crushed to a smooth paste with salt

375g packet puff pastry

Beaten egg, to glaze

Extra plums, to garnish

Serves 5

❶ Heat the oven to 190°C/375°F/Gas 5.

❷ Mix the garlic and plums and place in the cavity of the lamb.

❸ Roll up and sew the opening with a trussing needle and fine string.

❹ Cook in the oven, allowing 25 minutes per pound, plus 25 minutes.

❺ Remove from the oven and cool for approximately 1 hour. Remove the string carefully, without undoing the roll.

❻ Roll out the pastry and trim to 36cm.

❼ Place the lamb in the centre and fold the pastry around the joint, brushing with a little beaten egg to seal the joints.

❽ Turn the lamb over and place on a lightly greased baking sheet.

❾ Cut pastry leaves to decorate and brush with egg glaze.

❿ Cook in a hot oven 200°C/400°F/Gas 6 for about 30 minutes, until golden brown. Cover with foil and reduce the heat to 160°C/325°F/Gas 3 for a further 30 minutes.

⓫ Garnish with plum halves and serve with gravy made from the roasting juices.

SALT MARSH WELSH LAMB BAKED WITH POTATOES

Available all along the Welsh coast, salt marsh lamb is a speciality in Wales. It's the distinctive flavour, darker coloured meat and meltingly tender texture which make it significantly different from mountain lamb. In Wales, it is often enjoyed with a sauce made from seaweed or laverbread.

SALT MARSH WELSH LAMB BAKED WITH POTATOES

Ingredients

1.5kg leg of lamb, salt marsh if possible

3 garlic cloves, peeled and cut into slivers

2 tablespoons olive oil

Salt and black pepper

1 tablespoon chopped fresh herbs

900g potatoes

225g onions

1 large glass of dry white wine

2 tablespoons white wine vinegar

Juice of 1 lemon

Sprigs of rosemary

For the sauce:

100g laverbread

Juice of 1 orange

Knob of butter

Serves 4

① Insert garlic slivers into the surface of the lamb. Mix together the oil, seasoning and fresh herbs and pour over the surface of the lamb. Let the lamb marinate in the oil for an hour. Scatter over some rosemary.

② Sit the lamb on a wire rack over a roasting tin and pour the remaining herb oil marinade over the top. Roast at 220°C/425°F/Gas 7 for 15 minutes. Meanwhile, put the wine, vinegar and lemon juice into a pan and bring to the boil.

③ Peel the potatoes and onions and cut into largish chunks. Arrange them underneath the lamb on the rack and pour about half of the wine and vinegar mixture over the lamb.

④ Turn the heat down to 190°C/375°F/Gas 5 and continue to cook for 1 hour 15-30 minutes.

⑤ Baste from time to time with the remaining wine and vinegar mixture, turning the potatoes and onions to ensure they are cooked evenly.

For the sauce:

⑥ In a small pan, gently heat the laverbread, orange juice and knob of butter to make a rich sauce, adjusting the texture with some juices from the roasting pan.

WELSH LAMB SHANKS WITH THYME

This is the perfect casserole to prepare in advance and reheat the following day. The flavours improve and you can feed a hungry crowd, having done all the preparation ahead. Double up the quantities for a party of 8.

WELSH LAMB SHANKS WITH THYME

Ingredients

4 lamb shanks

1 large onion, sliced

2 carrots, peeled and sliced

2 sticks of celery, chopped

1 garlic clove, crushed

Handful of fresh thyme

¼ bottle white wine

Salt and freshly ground black pepper

Topping:

1 tablespoon chopped parsley

Grated rind of 1 lemon

1 garlic clove, crushed

Serves 4

❶ In a large, ovenproof casserole, fry the lamb shanks fast to brown all over.

❷ Remove the lamb from the pan, add the onion, carrots, celery and garlic and cook until they colour.

❸ Add the thyme, white wine and seasoning and boil up well. Return the lamb to the pan, cover and cook very slowly, on a low heat, for approximately 2 hours, until the meat is tender. Leave to cool and chill overnight.

❹ The next day, remove any fat from the top and place the lamb in a covered dish. Heat in the oven at 180°C/350°F/ Gas 5 for half an hour, or until the juices are bubbling right through.

❺ Sprinkle over the topping just before serving.

WELSH SPRING LAMB WITH ASPARAGUS

This is such a clever recipe. I often think that spring lamb has too delicate a flavour for a strong mint sauce, but served with spring asparagus the flavours of both lamb and asparagus come through really well.

WELSH SPRING LAMB WITH ASPARAGUS

Ingredients

900g asparagus

1 tablespoon olive oil

25g butter

900g lean lamb, trimmed and diced into 2.5cm cubes

4 small onions, or shallots, roughly chopped

1 tablespoon flour

150ml double cream

Salt and freshly ground black pepper

Lemon juice, to taste

Serves 4

1 Cook the asparagus in 300ml water until tender. Strain off the juice and reserve.

2 Cool the asparagus quickly, cut off the tips and keep to one side, then liquidize or blend the stems and sieve to make a pureé.

3 Heat the oil and butter in a large, heavy-based casserole.

4 Fry the lamb briskly with the chopped onions. Stir in the flour and cook for a minute, then gradually stir in the liquid in which the asparagus was cooked. Cover and cook the lamb for about 50 minutes, until tender. During cooking, skim off any fat from the surface of the liquid.

5 Stir in the asparagus pureé and cream, season and add lemon juice to sharpen.

6 Serve hot, garnished with the reserved asparagus tips, and with new potatoes tossed in butter and chopped fresh mint.

SLOW ROAST WELSH LAMB WITH A MUSTARD GLAZE

"The woman next door was very civil, and gave me a shoulder of lamb, with a lesson in cooking, as though I had watched my mother for more than two years for nothing." A great quote from How Green Was my Valley by Richard Llewellyn.

SLOW ROAST WELSH LAMB WITH A MUSTARD GLAZE

Ingredients

3kg lamb, shoulder or leg

6 tablespoons mustard

1 tablespoon cayenne pepper

5 tablespoons light muscovado sugar

1 tablespoon salt

1 tablespoon vegetable oil

Serves 4

1 Remove the bone from the lamb if you want to make the carving process easier.

2 Mix the mustard, pepper, sugar, salt and oil.

3 Pour over the lamb and leave to marinade for at least 2 hours in the fridge.

4 Cook at 180°C/350°F/ Gas 4 for 3-4 hours, basting with the juices at times, and turning the meat over after a couple of hours.

5 Cut the lamb into slices and serve with a mixture of seasonal vegetables. Or, for a family meal in the garden, just fold slices of the lamb into fresh baps.

LOIN OF WELSH LAMB
IN A CRISP ROLL

I have been preparing this recipe for years and years and it is always an absolute favourite. Although it takes a little time to prepare, once the lamb is ready for the oven your job is done.

LOIN OF WELSH LAMB IN A CRISP ROLL

Ingredients

1kg loin of lamb, boned and ready to roll

3 tablespoons sunflower oil

Stuffing:

1 tablespoon fresh herbs

½ orange rind, grated

1 garlic clove, crushed

Coating:

Beaten egg

Flour

Breadcrumbs

Sauce:

½ onion, finely chopped

1-2 tablespoons oil

1 tablespoon plain flour

300ml good lamb stock

Juice of ½ orange

3 tablespoons red wine

1 tablespoon redcurrant jam or marmalade

Salt and pepper

Serves 4

❶ Make up 300ml of good stock from the lamb bones.

❷ Spread the herbs, orange rind and garlic over the meat and roll up. Sew up using a trussing needle and fine string, then dip the lamb in flour, egg, then breadcrumbs to form a crust.

❸ Heat the oil in a roasting tin before putting in the meat.

Roast for an hour at 200°C/400°F/Gas 6, turning the lamb every fifteen minutes so that the roll crisps on all sides.

For the sauce:

❹ Gently cook the onion until soft, then allow it to brown. Stir in the flour and cook through before adding the stock and remaining ingredients. Simmer for 20 minutes then strain and taste, adding more seasoning and orange juice if needed.

❺ Remove the stitching from the lamb, slice onto a serving dish and serve the sauce separately.

WELSH LAMB CHOPS
WITH CRUSHED
MINTED PEAS

This is the ultimate quick and easy meal, simply buy the best lamb you can find. For milder spring lamb, the peas and mint make the perfect accompaniment.

WELSH LAMB CHOPS WITH CRUSHED MINTED PEAS

Ingredients

8 lamb chops

500g peas, fresh or frozen

6 mint leaves, finely chopped

1 tablespoon olive oil

Salt and freshly ground black pepper

Redcurrant jelly, to serve

Serves 4

1 Grill or griddle the lamb chops, at a high to moderate heat, for about 7 minutes each side. Alternatively, bake on a baking sheet in a hot oven for 15 minutes.

2 Cook the peas and drain.

3 Mash the peas together with the chopped mint leaves, olive oil and seasoning.

4 Arrange the cooked chops on top of the crushed peas with some redcurrant jelly on the side.

SKEWERS OF WELSH LAMB

This may seem like a recipe suitable for the Middle East, but remember that spices have been imported into Liverpool docks for centuries and would have found their way into Wales some time ago. The yoghurt marinade really does add a great tang to these delicious kebabs.

SKEWERS OF WELSH LAMB

Ingredients

500g lamb leg meat

6 tablespoons natural yoghurt

2 teaspoons turmeric

1 teaspoon coriander

Grated rind and juice of ½ lemon

2 tablespoons oil

1 garlic clove, crushed

1 red pepper, deseeded and cut into 8 pieces

1 red-skinned onion, cut into 8 wedges

Serves 4

1. Cut the lamb meat into 16 pieces.

2. Blend the yoghurt with the turmeric, coriander, lemon rind and juice, oil and garlic.

3. Stir in the meat, then cover and keep in a cool place for a minimum of 30 minutes so the flavours are absorbed.

4. Thread the meat, pepper and onion onto 4 skewers, starting and ending with lamb.

5. Cook the kebabs on a barbecue or under the grill for 15-20 minutes or to taste, turning often until brown and cooked through.

6. Brush any remaining marinade over the kebabs as they cook.

7. Serve with lemon wedges and rice.

BUTTERFLIED WELSH LAMB ON THE BARBECUE

Once the weather warms up and your barbecue is ready, this whole leg of lamb, barbecued quickly over the glowing embers, really does make the very best of what is the most delicious of meats.

BUTTERFLIED WELSH LAMB ON THE BARBECUE

Ingredients

1.6-1.8kg leg of lamb, boned. Either remove the bones from the leg of lamb in one piece, or ask your butcher

3 tablespoons olive oil

2 tablespoons dark soy sauce

2 tablespoons light muscovado sugar

Juice of 1 lemon

2.5cm fresh root ginger, peeled and finely grated

4 garlic cloves, peeled and halved

Freshly ground black pepper

Serves 4

1 Mix the oil, soy sauce, sugar, lemon juice, ginger and garlic. Place in a large dish or large plastic bag. Season the lamb with lots of ground black pepper on both sides and place into the marinade. Turn a couple of times, then cover or seal the bag and chill for 2-4 hours, turning once or twice.

2 Remove lamb from the marinade and cook on the barbecue for 35-45 mins, turning occasionally until done to taste. Alternatively, roast the butterflied lamb in the oven at 200°C/400°F/Gas 6 for about an hour.

3 Remove from the barbecue, cover and rest in a warm place for 15 mins before carving.

4 Serve with salad and minted new potatoes.

LAMB GUARD OF HONOUR WITH ROSEMARY AND PORT SAUCE

This can take a bit of time to prepare, and the sauce needs to have a well developed flavour, but the result is spectacular and well worth doing for a special event.

LAMB GUARD OF HONOUR WITH ROSEMARY AND PORT SAUCE

Ingredients

2 x 500g prepared best end racks of lamb, French trimmed

1 tablespoon finely chopped rosemary

1 tablespoon oil

Sauce:

1 tablespoon plain flour

200ml fresh lamb stock, hot

3 tablespoons ruby port

2 tablespoons redcurrant jelly

2 teaspoons lemon juice

Garnish:

1 good sprig rosemary

1 tablespoon chopped parsley

Serves 4

1 Preheat oven to 230°C/450°F/Gas 8.

2 Mix the rosemary with the oil and rub over the racks of lamb. Season with salt and pepper and link the racks together in a roasting tin. Cover the ends of the ribs with foil.

3 Roast for 25-30 minutes, depending on how pink you like your lamb. Once cooked, transfer to a warm dish, cover with foil and leave to rest for 10 mins.

For the sauce:

4 Pour away excess fat from the roasting tin, leaving about a tablespoon. Heat the pan gently, and stir in the flour. Cook for 30 seconds, then gradually stir in the stock and leave to simmer for a few minutes until reduced to a well-flavoured gravy, stirring well.

5 Add the port and redcurrant jelly and simmer again until the sauce has reduced well, then add the lemon juice. Strain into a sauce jug.

6 Arrange the lamb on a carving dish, accompanied by the sprig of rosemary and with the tips of the lamb rib bones dusted with chopped parsley.

METRIC AND IMPERIAL EQUIVALENTS

Weights	Solid
15g	½oz
25g	1oz
40g	1½oz
50g	1¾oz
75g	2¾oz
100g	3½oz
125g	4½oz
150g	5½oz
175g	6oz
200g	7oz
250g	9oz
300g	10½oz
400g	14oz
500g	1lb 2oz
1kg	2lb 4oz
1.5kg	3lb 5oz
2kg	4lb 8oz
3kg	6lb 8oz

Volume	Liquid
15ml	½ floz
30ml	1 floz
50ml	2 floz
100ml	3½ floz
125ml	4 floz
150ml	5 floz (¼ pint)
200ml	7 floz
250ml	9 floz
300ml	10 floz (½ pint)
400ml	14 floz
450ml	16 floz
500ml	18 floz
600ml	1 pint (20 floz)
1 litre	1¾ pints
1.2 litre	2 pints
1.5 litre	2¾ pints
2 litres	3½ pints
3 litres	5¼ pints

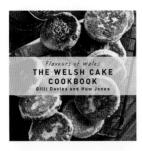

FLAVOURS OF WALES COLLECTION

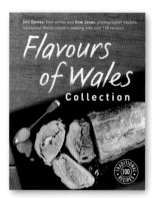

Cook up a Welsh feast with the full *Flavours of Wales* collection, in cookbooks, pocket books and notecards to share with friends.

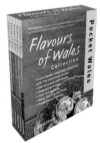

Flavours of Wales Collection book with over 100 recipes by Gilli Davies, photographed by Huw Jones **£20.00**

10 Recipe Notecards and envelopes in a gift pack. Full recipe inside with space for a message **£8.99**

Flavours of Wales Collectio in a gift slip case with 5 poc books **£12.99**

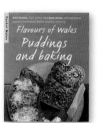

Flavours of Wales pocket books **£2.99**

Available from all good bookshops, kitchen and gift shops and online
www.graffeg.com Tel 01554 824000.

GRAFFEG

Books and Gifts from Wale